SCHOLASTIC
Time-to-Discover
READERS

Bears

Melvin and Gilda Berger

SCHOLASTIC INC.
New York Toronto London Auckland Sydney
Mexico City New Delhi Hong Kong Buenos Aires

Photographs: Cover: Jeff Lepore/Photo Researchers, New York; p. 1: Mark Newman/Bruce Coleman Inc., New York; p. 3: Jeff Lepore/Photo Researchers; p. 4: Dr. Eckart Pott/Bruce Coleman Inc.; p. 5: Erwin & Peggy Bauer/Bruce Coleman Inc.; p. 6: Tee Balog/Photo Researchers; p. 7: Erwin & Peggy Bauer/Bruce Coleman Inc.; p. 8: Tom McHugh/Photo Researchers; p. 9: Erwin & Peggy Bauer/Bruce Coleman Inc.; p. 10: Wayne Lankinen/Bruce Coleman Inc.; p. 11: Leonard Lee Rue III/Bruce Coleman Inc.; p. 12: Alan & Sandy Carey/Photo Researchers; p. 13: Mark Newman/Bruce Coleman Inc., New York; p. 14: Jeff Lepore/Photo Researchers; p. 15: Erwin & Peggy Bauer/Bruce Coleman Inc.; p. 16: Erwin & Peggy Bauer/Bruce Coleman Inc.

Book Design by Annette Cyr

ISBN 0-439-44533-7

21 20 19 18 17 16 15 14 13   7 8 9/0

Printed in the U.S.A.
First printing, October 2002

It is fall.

Bears eat fish.

Fun Fact
Bears eat both plants and animals.

Bears also eat berries.

Bears eat and eat and eat.

Fun Fact

Bears eat as much as they can in the fall. They will not eat much in the winter.

Many bears grow fat.

It is winter.

Fun Fact
Bears' homes
are called dens.

Bears live in dens.

Fun Fact

Sometimes bears wake up and leave their dens to look for food.

Bears sleep most of the time during winter.

Bear cubs are born.

It is spring.

Fun Fact
Cubs leave their dens after about 2 months, but they live with their mother for 1 or 2 years.

The bear cubs go out to play.

It is summer.

Bears climb trees.

This bear found something good to eat!